CONTENTS

FOREWORD

I'm Martin L. Eden, and this book is my exploration into how artificial intelligence can be a powerful ally in the world of writing and self-publishing. Through the process of creating this guide, I've leaned heavily on tools like ChatGPT, among others, to not only craft content but to demonstrate the practical applications of AI in a field that is as ancient as it is evolving. This isn't just a collection of insights; it's a reflection of my journey and experimentation with AI, designed to be as much a resource for discovery as it is a manual for action.

In these pages, you'll discover not just a book, but a companion for your journey into using AI to elevate your writing, streamline your publishing process, and navigate the path to financial and creative fulfillment. It's crafted for anyone—be you a novice writer, a seasoned author, or a curious mind—eager to harness the capabilities of AI for more efficient publishing and to explore the frontiers of emerging technology.

The landscape of self-publishing is vast and ever-changing, and while there are numerous guides out there, I've endeavored to make this one stand out by focusing on practicality. This isn't just theory; it's the practice of publishing in the digital age, underscored by the tools and techniques I've personally used to bring this very book into your hands. From the nuances of crafting a narrative with AI to the intricacies of optimizing your work for the market, each chapter is imbued with insights born from real-world application.

I'm excited about the future of self-publishing and the role AI plays in it. This book is a wonderful resource, rich with researched tools, links, and examples that have not only informed its creation but are also designed to guide you through your own publishing endeavors. It's a humble offering, yet one I hope you'll find concise, practical, and to the point—a primer replete with actionable advice and a treasure trove of resources to spark your curiosity and propel your projects forward.

There are indeed other books on the market covering similar themes, but I hold a hopeful conviction that this one carves its niche by providing you with a direct, useful introduction to integrating AI into your creative process. My goal is for this guide to serve as your springboard into the possibilities that AI and self-publishing hold, empowering you to write more compellingly, publish more efficiently, and succeed more spectacularly.

Warmly,

Martin L. Eden

INTRODUCTION

Welcome to a new era in publishing—an era where the boundaries of creativity and technology blur to unveil unprecedented opportunities for authors around the globe. *"AI Editor: Transforming Words into Wealth"* is your guide in navigating this changing landscape. Here, Artificial Intelligence (AI) is not just a tool, but a partner in the creative process of writing and publishing.

The advent of AI in the realm of self-publishing is revolutionizing the way we approach the written word. AI technologies offer abilities that were once only for a select few, including generating ideas, making drafts, editing, cover design, marketing, and market analysis. Now, these powerful tools are accessible to every writer, promising to democratize the art of publishing and opening doors to a future where the only limit is one's imagination.

This book is more than just a guide; it's a journey into the heart of this revolution. Whether you are an aspiring author dreaming of publishing your first book, or a seasoned writer looking to use new technologies, or just a curious enthusiast eager to explore- you are in the right place. AI is changing publishing, it will redefine being an author, and it offers paths to success that match the demands of the digital age.

In this guide, we will explore how AI can spark creativity and how it can help you speed up publishing and improve your final product. However, the promise of AI in publishing is not just about making tasks easier or more efficient- it's about amplifying human potential and opening up new avenues for creativity and expression. It's about turning *Words into Wealth*. It's not just about money, but also knowledge, experience, and connection, and you get all of these things from sharing your stories effectively with your audience.

So, welcome to the AI revolution in publishing! Your journey to becoming an *AI-empowered author* starts here. Let's turn the page and start this adventure together.

What to Expect from This Book

As you embark on the journey of "*AI Editor: Transforming Words into Wealth*," you are setting the course for an exploration of the intersection between emerging technology and self-publishing. This book is crafted to serve as a simple toolkit for authors at any stage of their journey, guiding you through the sometimes intricate landscapes of AI tools and self-publishing. Here's what you can expect from the pages that lie ahead:

A Comprehensive Guide: From the foundational concepts of AI to the practical application of AI tools in writing, editing, designing, publishing, and marketing your book, this guide covers it all. You'll gain a holistic understanding of how AI can be integrated into every step of the publishing process, enhancing your workflow and creative output.

Practical Insights and Strategies: This book is packed with actionable advice, step-by-step strategies and examples that demystify the use of AI in self-publishing. Whether it's choosing the right AI tools, tips for effective prompting, optimizing your manuscript with AI editing, or leveraging AI for marketing success, you'll find simple, practical insights that you can apply to your publishing endeavors.

Ethical and Creative Considerations: As we delve into the capabilities of AI, we also explore the ethical considerations and creative challenges that come with it. Learn how to maintain the authenticity of your voice and work within the ethical boundaries of AI usage, ensuring your work remains uniquely yours while benefiting from AI's power.

Future Trends: The world of AI is ever-evolving, and this book provides a glimpse into the future of AI in publishing. Stay ahead of the curve with insights into emerging trends, technologies, and how you can prepare for the next wave of innovation in the publishing industry.

Resources and Tools: Beyond the rich narrative and guidance, you'll find a curated list of resources and tools that can jump-start your journey. From AI writing assistants to design tools, marketing platforms, and community forums, this book acts as a gateway to a wealth of resources that will support your publishing journey.

Inspiration and Empowerment: Above all, this book is designed to inspire and empower you to embrace AI in your creative process.

It's a testament to the potential of combining human creativity with machine intelligence to create works that resonate with readers and stand the test of time.

At the heart of this guide is the promise to introduce you to AI tools that can transform your writing process. From developing your initial idea to polishing your final manuscript, AI can streamline these steps, making them more efficient and effective. You'll learn how to use AI to refine your narrative, enhance character development, and ensure your manuscript is error-free and ready for the world.

Beyond practical advice and technical insights, this book aims to inspire confidence in your abilities as an author. It encourages you to embrace AI as a creative partner, empowering you to reach new heights in your writing career.

By the end of *"AI Editor: Transforming Words into Wealth,"* you will not only have a comprehensive understanding of how to effectively use AI in your publishing journey but also the confidence to apply these tools creatively and ethically. Whether you're aiming to publish your first book or looking to leverage AI in your established writing process, this book is your guide to navigating the exciting possibilities that AI brings to the world of self-publishing. Let this be the catalyst that transforms your writing dreams into published reality, as you join the ranks of authors leading the charge in the AI revolution in publishing.

CHAPTER 1: A BRIEF OVERVIEW OF SELF PUBLISHING

You're likely already familiar with the concept of self-publishing. It's transformed from a niche avenue into a formidable force within the literary world, empowering authors globally. This shift isn't just about the technological strides we've made but also reflects a deeper change in how we value autonomy and direct access in the publishing process. As we delve into self-publishing, it's crucial to appreciate its pivotal role in the grander scheme of publishing in our digital era. This understanding sets the perfect backdrop for exploring how artificial intelligence (AI) is weaving itself into this vibrant tapestry.

Self-publishing has democratized the way stories are told and heard, breaking down the gates that once kept many authors on the outskirts. It's opened a world where the barriers to entry are not so much about who you know but about how you navigate the process and connect with your audience. But, as you might well know, with great power comes great responsibility. Self-publishing thrusts upon you the roles of writer, editor, designer, and marketer. While daunting, this also opens up unparalleled opportunities for creativity, higher earnings, and a direct line to your readers.

Thankfully, technology is on our side. Many aspects of self-publishing have been streamlined by new tools and platforms, from editing tools that polish your prose to platforms that bring your book to readers around the globe. And now, AI is stepping onto the scene, promising to revolutionize this process even further.

As we transition into discussing AI's role in self-publishing, remember: you're already on the front lines of a literary revolution. With AI, the possibilities for enhancing your work, simplifying complex tasks, and reaching readers are about to expand exponentially. Let's explore together how these new tools can elevate your self-publishing journey to new heights.

The Evolution and Impact of Self-Publishing

Democratizing the Publishing Process: Self-publishing has demolished the traditional barriers to entry in the publishing world, enabling authors to take control of the entire publishing process. This democratization has led to an explosion of new content, allowing diverse voices and stories to reach audiences directly in different formats and on different platforms.

Challenges and Opportunities: While self-publishing offers unparalleled freedom, it also presents new challenges. Authors must navigate the complexities of editing, design, distribution, and marketing on their own or seek out resources and professionals to assist in these areas. Despite these hurdles, the opportunities for creative control, higher royalties, and direct reader engagement make self-publishing an attractive option for many writers.

Practical Steps for Self-Publishing: An Overview

The self-publishing process transforms a manuscript into a book that's ready for readers' eyes. This overview walks through the essential steps, highlighting where AI can play a role—a theme we'll explore in depth later in the book.

Manuscript Preparation and Editing:
Your journey begins with manuscript preparation, where your initial drafts are honed into polished prose. AI can assist here, offering grammar and style suggestions through advanced editing software. While AI tools provide a good starting point for cleaning up your text, the nuanced touch of a professional editor ensures your manuscript's quality.

Formatting and Design:
After editing, your book needs formatting for print and digital versions, and an eye-catching cover design. AI has begun to revolutionize this step too, with design software offering AI-generated layout and cover suggestions based on genre and trends. However, many authors still prefer the personalized touch of a professional designer to bring their book's visual elements to life.

Choosing a Publishing Platform:

Selecting the right platform is critical for your book's distribution. Whether it's Amazon Kindle Direct Publishing (KDP), Barnes & Noble Press, or another, AI can help analyze each platform's potential reach and profitability for your specific genre. This insight can guide your decision, helping you choose the best platform(s) for your work.

Publication:

The publication process involves uploading your book files, setting a price, and officially publishing your book. Here, AI-driven analytics can optimize your book's metadata (title, description, keywords) to improve its visibility and appeal to your target audience, significantly impacting your book's discoverability.

Marketing and Promotion:

Marketing is where the self-published author often invests significant effort. AI can streamline this process, from identifying your target audience to optimizing ad placements on social media and search engines. Tools powered by AI offer data-driven insights to refine your marketing strategies, ensuring your book reaches its intended readers.

Post-Publication:

The work doesn't stop once your book is out. Gathering reviews, engaging with readers, and monitoring sales are ongoing tasks. AI tools can help track your book's performance across platforms, offering analytics that inform future marketing efforts and even guide your next writing project.

Each step of the self-publishing journey benefits from the integration of AI, simplifying tasks that once demanded considerable time and resources. As we delve deeper into this book, we'll explore how AI specifically enhances each of these areas, offering practical advice and innovative solutions to leverage technology in bringing your stories to life.

As this overview suggests, self-publishing is a vibrant and evolving field, offering a plethora of opportunities for authors willing to navigate its challenges. With the advent of AI, the potential for innovation and efficiency in self-publishing is boundless, promising an exciting future for authors and readers alike. As we delve deeper into the integration of AI in self-publishing, keep in mind this foundation of understanding, ready to explore how AI tools and technologies can amplify your success in the self-publishing worl

CHAPTER 2: THE BASICS OF AI

In the realm of publishing, artificial intelligence (AI) is no longer just a buzzword or a futuristic concept—it's a present-day tool that is reshaping the landscape for authors, editors, and publishers alike. But what exactly is AI, and how does it apply to the craft of writing and publishing? This chapter aims to demystify AI, providing a foundational understanding that will prepare you for integrating these technologies into your publishing journey.

◆ ◆ ◆

An Overview of Artificial Intelligence (AI)

What is AI?: At its core, artificial intelligence refers to the simulation of human intelligence processes by machines, especially computer systems. These processes include learning (the acquisition of information and rules for using the information), reasoning (using rules to reach approximate or definite conclusions), and self-correction. In the context of writing and publishing, AI can perform tasks such as generating content, suggesting improvements in writing, automating repetitive tasks, and providing insights based on data analysis.

"Artificial intelligence is not a substitute for human intelligence; it is a tool to amplify human creativity and ingenuity." – Fei-Fei Li

How does AI work?: AI operates through algorithms and models that allow it to process vast amounts of data, learn from it, and make predictions or decisions based on that learning. For authors, this means AI tools can analyze your writing style, suggest edits, help with plot development, and even predict what readers might enjoy based on current trends.

"I believe AI is going to change the world more than anything in the history of humanity. More than electricity." – Kai-Fu Lee

How do I use AI?: Let's break down some practical steps and explanations for beginners on how you might engage with AI in your writing process, focusing on prompting, iteration, and the conversational nature of interacting with AI models:

Prompting > Iteration > Conversation

- *Prompting*

The first step in utilizing AI for writing is learning how to prompt the model effectively. Think of prompting as asking a highly knowledgeable assistant for help. You can prompt AI with specific requests like, "Generate an outline for a mystery novel set in Victorian England," or ask for more general guidance, such as "Suggest ways to improve the pacing of my story." The key is to be clear and concise in your request, giving the AI a solid starting point to generate useful responses.

- *Iteration and Refinement*

AI-generated content often requires iteration and refinement. The initial output from your prompt might not be perfect, but it serves as a starting point. You can refine the AI's responses by providing feedback or asking follow-up questions. For example, if the AI suggests a plot twist you don't like, you might respond with, "Suggest a different twist that involves the main character's secret being revealed." This iterative process helps tailor the AI's output to better fit your vision.

- *Having a Conversation with the Model*

Interacting with AI in your writing process can be thought of as having a conversation with the model. This means not just asking for input and taking it verbatim but engaging with the AI's suggestions critically. Ask follow-up questions, challenge its proposals, and combine its ideas with your creativity. Over time, you'll become more adept at steering these conversations to get the most out of the AI, enhancing your writing in ways you might not have initially imagined.

Practical Steps to Get Started

1. Choose an AI Writing Tool: Select an AI tool or platform that suits your needs, whether it's for brainstorming, editing, or plot development.

2. Experiment with Prompts: Spend some time experimenting with different types of prompts to see how the AI responds. This will help you understand the tool's capabilities and limitations.

3. Incorporate AI Suggestions: Use the AI's output as a brainstorming tool or a draft to work from. Remember, the AI's suggestions are a starting point, not the final word.

4. Iterate Based on Feedback: Refine the AI's output by providing specific feedback or asking for alternatives. This iterative process is crucial for fine-tuning the content to your preferences.

5. Blend AI with Your Creativity: The most effective use of AI in writing comes from combining its suggestions with your unique voice and creativity. Let the AI inspire you, but keep your personal touch at the forefront of your work.

Types of AI Used in Publishing: There are several types of AI technologies that are particularly relevant for authors:

- *Natural Language Processing (NLP):* This technology enables AI to understand, interpret, and generate human language. NLP powers tools that can help with editing, summarizing content, and even generating whole sections of text.

- *Machine Learning (ML):* A subset of AI, ML enables systems to learn from data patterns and improve their performance over time without being explicitly programmed. ML can be used for predictive analysis, such as forecasting market trends or reader preferences.

- *Generative AI:* This includes tools like DALL-E for generating images and GPT (Generative Pretrained Transformer) for creating text. These can be used for cover design, promotional materials, and content creation.

Benefits of AI for Authors: The integration of AI into the publishing process offers numerous benefits:

- ***Efficiency:*** Automating tasks such as editing and formatting can save authors time, allowing them to focus more on creative aspects.

- ***Creativity:*** AI can inspire new ideas for stories, characters, or settings by generating suggestions based on a set of inputs.

- ***Personalization:*** AI can help tailor content to specific audiences, enhancing reader engagement.

- ***Market Insight:*** By analyzing trends and data, AI can provide valuable insights into what readers are currently interested in.

Ethical Considerations: As we embrace AI's potential, it's crucial to consider the ethical implications, such as ensuring originality in AI-generated content and maintaining transparency with readers about AI's role in the creative process.

As we venture deeper into the world of AI in self-publishing, remember that these technologies are tools designed to enhance your capabilities as an author. They offer exciting possibilities to streamline your workflow, elevate your writing, and connect more deeply with your audience. The journey into AI-assisted publishing is not just about keeping pace with technological advancements; it's about embracing new opportunities to tell your stories in ways that were previously unimaginable. Welcome to the future of writing—where AI is your ally in bringing your literary visions to life.

How AI Is Changing the Writing Landscape

The integration of artificial intelligence (AI) into the domain of writing and publishing is not just transforming the technical aspects of how books are produced and sold; it's revolutionizing the very essence of creative expression and authorship. This seismic shift is redefining the boundaries of what's possible, offering both challenges and unparalleled opportunities for authors. Let's explore the multifaceted impact of AI on the writing landscape.

Enhancing Creative Processes: AI is becoming an indispensable tool for many authors, aiding in the brainstorming process, suggesting plot twists, developing characters, or even generating entire narratives based on a set of parameters. Tools like ChatGPT have shown that AI can produce coherent and compelling text, sparking creativity in authors and providing a springboard for new ideas.

Streamlining Editing and Proofreading: The days of manual line-by-line editing, while still crucial, are being complemented by AI-powered tools that can catch grammatical errors, suggest stylistic improvements, and even help ensure consistency in character names and storylines. This not only speeds up the editing process but also elevates the quality of the final manuscript.

Personalized Content Creation: AI's ability to analyze vast amounts of data can help authors create content that resonates with specific audiences. By understanding reader preferences and market trends, AI can guide authors in tailoring their narratives, themes, and even marketing strategies to better align with their target demographic.

Accessibility and Democratization: AI tools are making writing more accessible, removing barriers for aspiring authors. Whether it's through providing writing assistance, automating the publishing process, or offering sophisticated marketing tools, AI is democratizing the ability to publish, promoting a more inclusive and diverse literary ecosystem.

Market Analysis and Trend Prediction: AI's prowess in data analysis is invaluable for understanding the ever-changing literary market. Authors can use AI to track trends, predict reader preferences, and make informed decisions about what to write next, potentially increasing their chances of success.

Challenges and Ethical Considerations: While the advantages are compelling, AI's role in writing also presents challenges. Issues of copyright, originality, and the ethical use of AI-generated content are at the forefront of discussions. As AI technology evolves, so too does the need for a balanced approach that respects creative integrity and copyright laws.

The Future of Authorship: As we look to the future, AI is set to continue its trajectory of innovation, blurring the lines between human and machine-generated content. The role of the author is expanding, with AI serving as both a collaborator and a tool that can unlock new forms of storytelling and reach wider audiences.

AI is not a replacement for human creativity but an augmentation of it. The use of AI in the writing process is a testament to the adaptability and resilience of human creativity, pushing the boundaries of what's possible in storytelling. As authors navigate this new landscape, the potential for AI to transform the writing process is limitless, offering a world where the art of storytelling can flourish in new and exciting ways. The AI revolution in writing is just beginning, and it promises to enrich the tapestry of human expression for generations to come.

CHAPTER 3: CHOOSING THE RIGHT AI TOOLS

In the ever-evolving landscape of artificial intelligence, a plethora of tools are available to assist writers in every phase of their journey—from conception to publication. Here's a broader look at some of the most impactful AI tools across various categories, offering alternatives and options to cater to diverse needs.

Section 1: Overview of AI Tools for Writers

Content Creation and Idea Generation

- *ChatGPT (OpenAI):* Excelling in generating text based on prompts, ChatGPT is invaluable for brainstorming, drafting, and overcoming creative blocks.

- *ShortlyAI:* Offers a focused environment for writing, with AI-driven suggestions to help flesh out stories or articles, making it ideal for writers seeking minimal distractions.

- *Jasper:* Known for its versatility in content generation, Jasper can assist in writing blog posts, social media content, and even book chapters with a user-friendly interface.

- *Sudowrite:* Sudowrite acts as a writing partner that offers suggestions, helps overcome writer's block, and refines prose. It's particularly useful for fiction and creative writing, providing synonyms, rewriting paragraphs, and suggesting plot developments.

- *Grammarly:* Grammarly is a widely-used tool for grammar checking, style improvement, and plagiarism detection. It uses NLP to understand the context of sentences, making it invaluable for editing and refining manuscripts.

- *INK:* INK is tailored for SEO content creation but is also useful for authors looking to optimize their online presence. It uses NLP and ML to suggest improvements that can increase a piece's visibility on search engines.

- *Quillbot:* Quillbot is a paraphrasing tool that helps rewrite sentences or paragraphs to enhance clarity or alter tone. It's beneficial for editing and refining content, ensuring readability and engagement.

- *Writesonic:* Writesonic specializes in marketing content creation, including landing pages, ad copy, and product descriptions. It can also assist authors in generating promotional materials and summaries for their books.

- *Writer:* Utilizes the Palmyra LLM, focusing on transparency and security. It's designed for legal compliance, style guide adherence, and offers a fact-checking feature to ensure content accuracy. This tool is particularly beneficial for companies looking to maintain a specific brand voice across all written content.

- *Rytr:* Known for its solid free plan and affordable high-volume options, Rytr includes basic AI art generation in every plan, making it a cost-effective choice for individuals and small businesses looking to explore AI-generated content and images.

- *Longshot AI:* Stands out for its fact-checking system, aiming to solve the issue of AI-generated content's accuracy. It's a complex software offering document editing, topic research, and quality of life tools to enhance content creation and ensure factual correctness.

- *Nyle AI:* Tailored for eCommerce businesses, Nyle AI uses GPT-3 to generate content focused on short-form copywriting. It includes over 15 short-form templates and features like an image enhancer and influencer research, providing a comprehensive toolkit for online store owners

Image Generation and Design

- *Dall-E:* Creates unique images from textual descriptions, useful for book covers and promotional materials.

- *Visme:* Known for its text-to-image generation tool, Visme offers a broad spectrum of output styles, including photos, paintings, pencil drawings, and more, making it a versatile choice for creators looking to merge AI graphics with content types like infographics and social media posts

- *Midjourney:* Distinguished by its ability to generate digital artwork that resembles hand-drawn illustrations rather than photorealistic images, Midjourney is perfect for creating 'pretty' images like gothic architecture and fantasy landscapes

- *Canva's Magic Write & Design with Text to Image:* Integrates AI-driven design and content creation, allowing for easy generation of marketing materials, social media graphics, and book covers with text-to-image features.

- *NightCafe AI:* Tailored for digital art creation, NightCafe AI offers detailed customization for AI-generated art, making it suitable for both beginners and experienced artists looking to explore digital creativity.

- *DeepArt:* Specializes in transforming photos into artworks based on various artistic styles, ideal for authors seeking distinctive visuals for their projects.

Editing and Proofreading

- *Grammarly:* Offers comprehensive feedback on writing errors, style, and tone improvements, suitable for a broad range of writing tasks.

- *Hemingway Editor:* Focuses on enhancing clarity and readability by identifying complex sentences and suggesting simplifications.

- *ProWritingAid:* Provides detailed writing reports, highlighting areas like repetitiveness, vague wording, sentence length variation, and more, making it a robust tool for in-depth editing.

- *Antidote:* Offers both online and local proofreading capabilities, supporting English and French. It's praised for its extensive reports and is a great choice for those concerned about privacy and data security.

- *Quillbot:* While primarily a paraphrasing tool, Quillbot also features a grammar checker and citation generator, making it useful for academic works and essays. It's celebrated for its ease of use and the range of tools beyond proofreading.

- *Ginger Software:* Provides a cost-effective option for proofreading, supporting 60 languages. It's beneficial for those needing a basic grammar and spell check across various devices.

- *WhiteSmoke:* Known for its affordability and support for 55 languages, WhiteSmoke offers a comprehensive solution that includes grammar and spelling checks. It works with most browsers and operating systems.

SEO and Content Optimization

- *MarketMuse:* Uses AI to analyze content and offer recommendations on how to improve for better search engine rankings and reader engagement.

- *SurferSEO:* Focuses on optimizing online content with real-time SEO guidelines, helping writers create more searchable and visible web content.

- *Clearscope:* Offers easy-to-use content optimization based on current SEO best practices, making it suitable for bloggers and content marketers.

- *Alli:* AI focuses on automating SEO tasks like meta tags optimization, link descriptions, and image alts, making it easier for SEO teams to manage campaigns without needing developers or coding knowledge. It integrates with popular content management systems, offering custom automation for on-page optimizations.

- *RankIQ:* suggests titles and content for posts, offering a list of high-traffic, low-competition keywords. It helps create blog post outlines quickly, aiming to rank your content on the first page of Google.

- *Frase:* simplifies SEO content research and optimization, helping users create thorough content briefs and compare their content to competitors'. It aims to make publishing Google-friendly content easier by providing an easy-to-use text editor and competitor analysis.

- *Diib:* offers growth plans and alerts for SEO, social, mobile, and visitor experience optimization. It provides competitor monitoring, keyword tracking, and new content ideas to enhance your SEO strategy.

- *Outranking:* Outranking automates content creation targeting organic traffic through SERP analysis. It provides tools for creating SEO-focused content, such as outlines, briefs, titles, and optimizing existing articles for better search engine performance

Marketing and Promotion

- *CopyAI:* An AI-powered tool designed to generate marketing copy and content ideas quickly, from email marketing to ad copy and product descriptions.

- *Writesonic:* Specializes in creating marketing content, including landing pages, ads, and emails, with specific templates for various marketing needs.

- *Lumen5:* A video creation platform that uses AI to transform text content into engaging video content, perfect for promotional efforts on social media.

- *Hootsuite's free AI tools*: offer a suite of content creation aids, including caption and bio writers, username idea generators, and AI hashtag generators, optimized for social media across multiple languages, making it ideal for content creators and small businesses starting their social media journey.

- *Persado Motivation AI*: An enterprise-level Generative AI platform, perfect for generating high-converting digital marketing messages. It personalizes messages to drive engagement, using a comprehensive knowledge base of consumer motivations and an experimentation engine for language and creative permutations.

- *Personalize:* Personalize leverages AI to track customer preferences, helping businesses promote the right products at the right time. Its real-time insights and personalized campaign capabilities can significantly boost email open rates and click rates.

Each of these tools represents a facet of the potential AI holds to streamline the writing, editing, publishing, and marketing processes for authors. By leveraging the specific strengths of these tools, writers can significantly enhance their productivity, creativity, and engagement with their audience, ensuring their work stands out in a crowded marketplace.

Selecting AI Tools That Fit Your Needs

Assess Your Goals: Before diving into the vast sea of AI tools, it's essential to clearly define what you aim to achieve with AI assistance. Are you looking to streamline your writing process, enhance creativity, improve the quality of your manuscript, or boost your marketing efforts? Your goals will dictate which tools are most suitable for you.

Consider Your Budget: AI tools range from free versions with basic functionalities to premium offerings with advanced features. Assess your budget to determine which tools you can afford while still meeting your needs. Remember, investing in the right tool can save time and improve the quality of your work, potentially leading to better sales and more opportunities.

Ease of Use: The best AI tool is the one you'll actually use. Test different tools to see which ones fit seamlessly into your workflow. Many AI tools offer trial periods, allowing you to explore their functionalities before making a commitment.

Integration with Your Workflow: Consider how well an AI tool integrates with other tools and platforms you're using. Compatibility can significantly affect your efficiency and productivity. For example, if you're using a specific writing software, look for AI tools that complement or integrate well with it.

Community and Support: The presence of a strong user community and reliable customer support can be invaluable, especially when you're learning to use a new tool. Look for tools that offer robust support resources, tutorials, and user forums.

By carefully considering your needs, goals, and resources, you can select AI tools that not only enhance your writing and publishing efforts but also make the journey more enjoyable and rewarding. Remember, the right AI tools should serve as extensions of your creativity, helping you to achieve results that were once out of reach.

CHAPTER 4: CRAFTING YOUR MANUSCRIPT WITH AI

In the journey of bringing a book to life, the initial stages of crafting your manuscript are pivotal. AI has the power to transform these early phases of writing, from conceptualizing your narrative structure to developing multifaceted characters. Let's explore how AI can be your ally in enhancing the foundational elements of your story and refining your manuscript to meet professional standards.

◆ ◆ ◆

Brainstorming with AI

Before we dive into enhancing narrative structure and character development, it's crucial to address the foundation of any writing project: brainstorming. This initial phase is where ideas are born, nurtured, and culled, and AI has emerged as a powerful ally in this creative process.

Idea Generation: AI tools can be instrumental in generating a plethora of ideas for your book. Whether you're looking for an intriguing plot for your next novel or a compelling subject for a non-fiction piece, AI can analyze existing literature and trends to suggest fresh, relevant topics.

Here are a few prompt templates designed to generate ideas for different types of writing projects:

- ***Fiction - Mystery/Thriller:***
"Generate a plot idea for a mystery novel set in a small coastal town where the main character uncovers secrets from their past while investigating a series of disappearances."

- ***Science Fiction/Fantasy:***
"Suggest a storyline for a science fiction novel that explores the impact of artificial intelligence on human relationships, set in a future where AI and humans coexist."

- ***Self-Help/How-To Guides:***
"Provide concepts for a self-help book focused on overcoming procrastination, including strategies that incorporate both

traditional practices and modern technological solutions."

● ***Historical Fiction:***

"Create a narrative foundation for a historical fiction piece set during the Renaissance period, centered around the invention of a revolutionary piece of technology and its effects on society."

● ***Non-Fiction - Biography:***

"Propose an outline for a biography of a lesser-known inventor whose creations changed the course of history, highlighting key moments in their life and the impact of their work."

● ***Children's Literature:***

"Generate ideas for a children's book series that teaches important life lessons through adventures of a group of animal friends in a magical forest, focusing on themes such as friendship, courage, and kindness."

These templates can be adjusted and tailored to fit specific interests or themes you wish to explore further. By providing AI with clear, detailed prompts, you can unlock a wide range of creative possibilities and discover unique angles for your writing projects.

Theme Exploration: With AI, you can explore various themes and how they might weave into your narrative, offering insights into complex subjects or suggesting new angles on familiar ideas.

Here are a few theme generation prompts for AI tools that cater to different types of writing projects:

● ***Fiction - Mystery/Thriller:***

"Identify a central theme for a mystery novel set in a small coastal town, focusing on the impact of hidden pasts on the present, and how secrets can shape or distort personal identities."

● ***Science Fiction/Fantasy:***

"Generate a theme for a science fiction novel that examines the ethical implications of AI in society, particularly how artificial intelligence challenges our understanding of what it means to be human and the boundaries of human empathy."

● ***Self-Help/How-To Guides:***

"Suggest a unifying theme for a self-help book on overcoming procrastination, emphasizing the journey from chaos to clarity and the transformation that structured time management brings to one's personal and professional life."

● ***Historical Fiction:***

"Propose a theme for a historical fiction piece set during the Renaissance, highlighting the tension between tradition and innovation, and how the pursuit of knowledge and artistic expression can drive societal change."

● ***Non-Fiction - Biography:***

"Outline a theme for a biography of a lesser-known inventor, focusing on the theme of recognition versus obscurity and exploring the idea that true innovation often goes unnoticed in its time but can leave a lasting impact on future generations."

● ***Children's Literature:***
"Create a series of themes for a children's book series set in a magical forest, such as the value of friendship, the courage to face fears, and the importance of kindness, illustrating how these virtues help overcome challenges."

These prompts are designed to help AI tools provide you with themes that not only serve as the backbone of your writing projects but also ensure they carry meaningful messages that resonate with your audience.

Title Creation: Finding the perfect title can be as challenging as writing the book itself. AI can help generate a list of potential titles based on your story's themes, characters, and plot, providing a creative springboard for your brainstorming session.

For generating book titles in the *Fiction - Mystery/Thriller* genre, you could use a prompt like this:
"Generate 6 intriguing titles for a mystery/thriller novel set in a small coastal town, where the protagonist uncovers secrets from their past while investigating a series of mysterious disappearances."

Based on this prompt suggestion, here are five potential titles generated by ChatGPT:

"Shadows Over Saltwater"

"The Tide of Forgotten Secrets"

"Echoes in the Fog"

"Whispers from the Deep"

"Vanished in the Veil"

Taking these title suggestions from AI is just the beginning of a collaborative creative process. Think of AI as a brainstorming partner that offers a starting point; it's up to you to add your unique touch, refine the ideas, and mold them into something that truly resonates with your vision and style. This iterative process, bouncing ideas back and forth between you and AI, enhances creativity, ensuring the final outcome is not only inspired by AI but is imbued with your personal flair and storytelling nuances.

AI's role in brainstorming is akin to having a conversation with a muse that has read every book in the library. By inputting your initial thoughts and ideas, you can engage in a dynamic dialogue with the AI, prompting it to suggest enhancements, alternatives, and sometimes, entirely new directions for your story. As we explore the subsequent sections on narrative structure, character development, and beyond, remember that AI's potential to aid in brainstorming is just the starting point. Its capabilities extend through every phase of writing, offering support, inspiration, and critical analysis to refine your manuscript into a masterpiece.

Enhancing Narrative Structure and Character Development

Narrative Structure: AI tools can play a significant role in shaping the structural integrity of your story. By analyzing successful books within your genre, AI can offer insights into effective pacing, plot progression, and the distribution of key narrative elements. Tools like ChatGPT can generate outlines or suggest plot twists, ensuring your story maintains momentum and engages readers from start to finish.

- *Plot Development:* Utilize AI to explore various plot scenarios and their potential impacts on your narrative. AI-generated suggestions can inspire creative directions you might not have considered, offering a broader palette of possibilities for your story's progression.

- *Character Arcs:* AI can assist in developing complex character arcs by suggesting motivations, conflicts, and resolutions that align with your story's themes. Tools like Character.AI allow for interactive dialogue with AI-generated characters, helping you understand their voices and perspectives more deeply.

Character Development: The depth of your characters significantly influences reader engagement. AI can suggest traits, backstories, and relationships, enriching your characters and making them more relatable.

For example, to generate suggestions for character development for the protagonist in a mystery/thriller novel set in a small coastal town, you might use the following prompt:

"Generate a character profile for the protagonist of a mystery/thriller novel set in a small coastal town, focusing on unique traits, a compelling backstory, and complex relationships that drive them to

uncover hidden secrets."

Based on this prompt suggestion, here is the very brief character profile generated by ChatGPT:

Name: *Alex Morgan*

Trait: *Inquisitive and resilient, with a keen eye for detail.*

Backstory: *Once a promising detective in a bustling metropolis, Alex's life took a sharp turn after a case gone wrong led to an unjust dismissal. Seeking solace and a fresh start, Alex moved to the quiet coastal town of Havenport, only to find that the serene facade hides deep, dark secrets.*

Relationships: *Alex quickly befriends the local librarian, Jamie, whose extensive knowledge of the town's history proves invaluable. However, Alex's probing nature stirs tension with the town's mayor, who seems to have something to hide.*

Drive: *Fueled by a desire for redemption and a quest for truth, Alex is determined to peel back the layers of deceit in Havenport, even if it means confronting their own demons.*

This character profile serves as a foundational piece, providing a solid basis for further development and integration into the novel's plot.

- *Dialogue Generation:* Crafting authentic dialogue can be challenging. AI tools can generate dialogue samples that capture your characters' unique voices, providing a foundation you can refine to enhance authenticity.

  Practical steps for generating dialogue with AI:
  1. Craft Your Prompt: Create a detailed prompt that includes the scenario where the dialogue takes place, the emotional

tone, and any specific information that needs to be conveyed in the conversation.

Example: "Generate a tense dialogue between a detective and a suspect in a small coastal town, where the detective subtly accuses the suspect without direct confrontation."

2. *Use Iterative Prompts*: After receiving the initial dialogue from the AI, you can refine it by providing feedback through iterative prompts. For instance, if the dialogue lacks tension, you could ask, "Intensify the suspicion in the detective's questions while maintaining a polite tone."

3. *Personalize and Edit:* Once you have a dialogue draft, personalize it further by adding unique speech patterns or slang that your characters might use. Use the AI-generated dialogue as a base and edit it to fit your story's voice and your characters' personalities.

4. *Contextual Integration:* Place the dialogue within your manuscript, ensuring it flows naturally with the surrounding narrative. Adjust any narrative elements if necessary to make the dialogue fit seamlessly.

5. *Review and Revise:* Finally, review the dialogue in the context of your overall story. Consider how it contributes to character development, plot advancement, and reader engagement. Make revisions as needed, either on your own or by soliciting additional suggestions from the AI tool.

Editing for Tone, Grammar, Style, and Coherence

Emotional Tone: AI's analysis of emotional tone can help ensure that your characters' emotions evolve naturally throughout the story, aligning with their experiences and the narrative's demands.

Grammar and Punctuation: The credibility of your manuscript is often judged by its adherence to grammar and punctuation rules. AI-powered tools like Grammarly and ProWritingAid can scan your text for errors, offering corrections and explanations to help you learn and avoid similar mistakes in the future.

Style and Voice: Maintaining a consistent style and voice is crucial for reader immersion. AI editing tools can analyze your writing to identify inconsistencies in tone or style, suggesting adjustments to align with your desired voice. Additionally, they can provide stylistic suggestions based on genre-specific writing conventions.

- ***Readability:*** Tools such as the Hemingway Editor evaluate your manuscript's readability, pointing out complex sentences and recommending simplifications without compromising your narrative's depth or complexity.

- ***Coherence and Flow:*** Ensuring that your story flows smoothly from one chapter to the next is essential for keeping readers engaged. AI can help identify areas where transitions are needed, suggest where to add clarifying information, or recommend rearranging sections for better narrative flow.

By integrating AI into the writing and editing processes, authors can achieve a level of polish and depth that resonates with readers and stands up to professional scrutiny. Whether you're sculpting the broad strokes of your narrative or refining the minute details of your prose, AI is an invaluable tool that can elevate your manuscript from good to exceptional.

CHAPTER 7: CHOOSING THE RIGHT PUBLISHING PLATFORMS

Selecting the right platform for your book is a decision that can significantly impact its success. With numerous options available, AI can help narrow down the best fit based on your book's genre, target audience, and your personal goals.

Comparing Self-Publishing Platforms

Overview of Major Platforms: Discuss the features, benefits, and limitations of major self-publishing platforms like Amazon

Kindle Direct Publishing (KDP), Barnes & Noble Press, Kobo Writing Life, and Apple Books for Authors. Consider aspects such as market reach, royalty rates, and format support.

Let's take a quick tour of some of the online self-publishing platforms available to authors today, each providing unique services to help bring your book directly to readers:

- *Apple Books for Authors:* Apple's self-publishing platform enables authors to publish e-books directly to the Apple Books Store, providing access to readers who use Apple devices.

- *Barnes & Noble Press:* This platform allows authors to publish both e-books and print-on-demand books, with distribution on Barnes & Noble's online store, giving authors access to millions of readers.

- *BookBaby:* A comprehensive service that provides e-book distribution, print-on-demand, and custom book printing, along with additional marketing and promotional services.

- *Draft2Digital:* Known for its user-friendly interface, Draft2Digital offers e-book and print book distribution to a network of online retailers and library services.

- *IngramSpark:* A favorite for authors looking to reach a wide audience, IngramSpark provides access to Ingram's extensive distribution network, which includes independent bookstores and libraries.

- *Kobo Writing Life:* Kobo offers an easy way for authors to publish e-books and reach readers in over 190 countries through the Kobo Books platform.

- *Lulu:* Offers various self-publishing services, including e-book and print-on-demand options, with the ability to reach audiences across multiple retailers.

- *Amazon Kindle Direct Publishing (KDP):* The largest and most popular platform for self-publishing e-books and paperbacks, offering worldwide distribution and the option for authors to earn up to 70% royalties on sales.

- *Reedsy:* An online platform that connects authors with professional editors, designers, and marketers to help prepare their book for self-publishing on various platforms.

- *Smashwords:* A veteran in the self-publishing domain, Smashwords offers distribution to major e-book retailers and provides authors with various tools for marketing and sales tracking.

Utilizing AI for Comparison: AI tools can compare these platforms based on real-time data, including user reviews, success stories within your genre, and platform policies that could affect your book's visibility and sales.

Utilizing AI to Select the Best Platform for Your Book

Analyzing Platform Data: Use AI to analyze sales data, reader demographics, and genre popularity across different platforms. This analysis can reveal where your book is likely to find its most receptive audience.

Matching Your Book to a Platform: Based on your target audience identification and market analysis, AI can recommend the platform(s) where your book fits best, considering factors like reader preferences for format (eBook, paperback, audiobook) and purchasing habits.

Optimizing for Multiple Platforms: If you decide to publish on multiple platforms, AI can help optimize your book's listing for each platform's specific requirements and audience characteristics, ensuring the best possible presentation and reach.

By methodically analyzing your genre, understanding your audience, and selecting the appropriate publishing platforms with the assistance of AI, you position your book for greater visibility, engagement, and success in the competitive world of self-publishing. This strategic approach allows you to leverage technology to make informed decisions that align with your publishing goals.

CHAPTER 5: CREATIVE DESIGN AND FORMATTING WITH AI

The presentation of your book plays a crucial role in attracting readers and ensuring a seamless reading experience. This chapter delves into how AI can revolutionize the creative design and formatting aspects of your book, turning these daunting tasks into streamlined, efficient processes.

◆ ◆ ◆

Using AI for Book Cover Design

Understanding the Importance of Your Cover: The cover is often the first interaction potential readers have with your book. It needs to communicate the essence of your story, attract attention, and stand out in a crowded market. AI can assist in creating a visually appealing cover that resonates with your target audience.

Step-by-Step Guide to AI-Generated Covers:

- ***Conceptualization:*** Start with a clear idea of your book's theme, genre, and tone. Use tools like ChatGPT to brainstorm cover concepts that align with your book's content and appeal to your target demographic.

  For example, you might use a prompt like this:

  "Create a cover design concept for a mystery/thriller novel set in a small coastal town, highlighting themes of secrets and redemption. The design should evoke suspense and intrigue, balancing dark and hopeful tones, to attract fans of classic mysteries and modern thrillers."

- ***Using AI Design Tools:*** Platforms like Canva integrate AI to offer design suggestions. Input your book's title, genre, and key themes to receive template suggestions. For more advanced AI-generated imagery, Dall-E and DeepArt can create custom illustrations based on textual descriptions you provide. Based on the suggested prompt above, Dall-E generated this image:

- ***Customization:*** Once you have a base design, customize it to fit your vision. Adjust colors, fonts, and layouts. AI tools often suggest variations, making it easy to explore different aesthetics. Also at this stage it can be helpful to determine the requirments for image dimensions- each publishing platform will require specific size, dimensions and file types for your cover artwork.

- ***Feedback and Iteration:*** Use AI feedback tools to analyze the cover's impact. Tools like Canva's Design Feedback can gauge attention areas and overall appeal. Iterate based on this feedback to enhance your cover's effectiveness.

Tips for Success:

- Keep your target audience in mind. Different genres have different cover conventions.

- Use high-contrast colors and readable fonts to ensure your cover stands out even in thumbnail size.

- Spend time looking at book covers and identify what features appeal to you, then try to incoporate these qualities into your own cover art.

Formatting Your Book with AI Assistance

The Role of Formatting in Reader Experience: Proper formatting ensures that your book is accessible and enjoyable to read, whether it's in print or digital form. Consistency in layout, typography, and design elements contributes to a professional appearance and reader satisfaction.

AI-Assisted Formatting Steps:
- ***Choosing the Right Tool:*** Tools like Vellum offer AI-assisted formatting, suggesting layouts and styles based on genre and current trends. Select a tool that caters to both eBooks and print formats for versatility.

- ***Inputting Your Manuscript:*** Upload your manuscript into the formatting software. AI algorithms analyze your text, suggesting chapter breaks, headers, and footers appropriate for your genre.

- ***Customization and Layout Design:*** Customize the suggested layout. AI tools can recommend font styles, sizes, and spacing that enhance readability and appeal to your genre's audience. Experiment with different layouts for chapter titles, margins, and spacing to find the perfect fit.
- ***Visual Elements:*** For adding images or decorative elements, AI can suggest placements that complement the text without disrupting the reading flow. Ensure any images are high resolution and relevant to the content.

- ***Preview and Adjust:*** Utilize the tool's preview feature to see how your book will appear in different formats. Pay attention to how chapters start, the spacing of text, and the overall ease of navigation. Make adjustments based on this preview to ensure a polished final product.

Tips for Success:

- Keep an eye on the details. Small inconsistencies can detract from the professional quality of your book.

- Consider the requirements of different platforms. Formatting needs can vary between print-on-demand services and eBook platforms.

By leveraging AI for both cover design and formatting, you can ensure your book not only captures attention but also provides a satisfying reading experience. These AI tools not only save time and resources but also empower you to maintain creative control over your book's presentation, making it possible to achieve professional-quality design and formatting without the need for extensive design experience.

CHAPTER 6: MARKET ANALYSIS AND TARGET AUDIENCE IDENTIFICATION

Understanding the market and identifying your target audience are crucial steps before publishing your book. These steps ensure that your book meets the expectations of your readers and stands out in a competitive market. Let's explore how to conduct a thorough market analysis and target audience identification with the help of AI.

Analyzing Your Genre and Market Trends

Leveraging AI for Market Research: AI tools can analyze large datasets to identify trends in your genre, including which topics are gaining popularity and what readers are currently interested in. Tools like Google Trends and MarketMuse can provide insights into search trends and content performance, respectively.

Step-by-Step Market Analysis:
- ***Define Your Genre:*** Clearly define the genre or genres your book fits into. This will narrow down your research scope and make your analysis more relevant.

- ***Use AI Tools to Gather Data:*** Utilize AI-powered tools to analyze the market. Look at sales data, reader reviews, and social media mentions to understand what works well in your genre.

- ***Identify Trends:*** Pay attention to emerging themes, character types, and plot structures that are resonating with readers. Also, note any saturation points—themes or concepts that may be overused. Use AI to help generate alternatives.

- ***Evaluate Your Findings:*** Assess how your book aligns with these trends. Are there gaps in the market your book could fill? Are there trends you can capitalize on or avoid?

Applying Insights to Your Book: Use the insights gained from your analysis to make informed decisions about your book's positioning, marketing strategy, and even content adjustments to better meet market demands.

Identifying and Understanding Your Target Audience

Building Reader Personas with AI: AI can help create detailed reader personas by analyzing online behavior, purchase history, and engagement with similar genres. Tools like HubSpot's Marketing

Hub utilize AI to segment audiences and predict preferences.

Steps to Identify Your Target Audience:
- ***Segment Your Potential Readers:*** Use AI to segment the market based on demographics, interests, and reading habits. This helps in creating a focused picture of your ideal reader.

- ***Analyze Reader Preferences:*** Dive into what your target audience prefers in terms of themes, pacing, character development, and storytelling techniques.

- ***Engage and Validate:*** Use social media and online forums to engage with potential readers. AI tools can help analyze responses to your queries, providing deeper insights into what your audience values.

Crafting Your Marketing Message: With a clear understanding of your target audience, tailor your book's marketing messages to speak directly to their preferences and needs, enhancing the effectiveness of your promotional efforts.

To effectively tailor your marketing messages for various platforms and promotional efforts, consider incorporating AI tools to enhance creativity and efficiency. Here are four AI-assisted messaging strategies:

1. AI-Enhanced Summary for Platform Page (e.g., Amazon, Goodreads): Use AI to generate a dynamic summary that encapsulates the essence of your mystery/thriller novel. AI can help identify key plot points and themes that resonate with readers, ensuring your summary is both captivating and informative.

Example:
"When secrets from the deep threaten to engulf the small coastal

town of Haven's End, only one person dares to confront them. 'Redemption's Tide' weaves a tale of mystery and courage in the face of darkness. Discover the power of secrets, and the price of redemption."

2. *AI-Crafted One-Line Description for Social Media:* Leverage AI to create concise, impactful one-liners perfect for engaging your audience on social media platforms. AI can analyze trending phrases and keywords to maximize appeal and click-through rates.

Example:
"Secrets surface, pasts collide—dive into 'Redemption's Tide' for a thrilling ride through Haven's End."

3. *Email Marketing Teaser with AI:* Utilize AI to personalize email teasers that resonate with your subscribers. AI can analyze subscriber data to tailor messages that align with their reading preferences, enhancing the connection and intrigue.

Example:
"Explore the shadows of Haven's End in 'Redemption's Tide'. Join me on a journey where every secret uncovered is a step closer to redemption—or ruin."

4. *AI-Optimized Ad Copy for Online Advertising:* Employ AI to refine your online ad copy, ensuring it's optimized for your target audience. AI tools can test different versions of your ad copy, analyze performance data, and suggest the most effective phrasing to capture attention and drive conversions.

Example:
"Unearth Haven's End darkest secrets in 'Redemption's Tide'. Where every whisper of the past has a price. Will redemption be enough?"

In each case, AI acts as a powerful collaborator, offering data-driven insights and creative suggestions that enhance the effectiveness of your marketing messages. By leveraging AI, you can ensure that your book's promotional efforts are not only creative but also strategically aligned with your target audience's preferences and behaviors

CHAPTER 8: DEVELOPING YOUR MARKETING STRATEGY WITH AI

In today's digital age, marketing your book effectively requires more than just traditional strategies. AI offers innovative tools and approaches to design and execute a marketing plan that captures attention, engages potential readers, and drives sales.

Creating an AI-Driven Marketing Plan

Identifying Marketing Goals with AI: Begin by defining clear, measurable goals for your marketing campaign. AI can analyze market data, competitor success stories, and your target audience to recommend specific objectives, such as increasing website traffic, boosting pre-order numbers, or enhancing email open rates.

Steps to Develop an AI-Driven Marketing Plan:
- ***Market Analysis:*** Use AI tools to perform a detailed analysis of the current market, identifying trends and opportunities in your genre.

- ***Audience Segmentation:*** Leverage AI to segment your audience more effectively based on their reading habits, preferences, and engagement patterns.

- ***Channel Selection:*** AI can help determine the most effective marketing channels (social media, email, blogs, etc.) for reaching your target audience by analyzing where similar books have found success.

- ***Content Strategy:*** Utilize AI to craft a content strategy that resonates with your audience, suggesting topics, formats, and messaging that are most likely to engage readers.

- ***Performance Tracking:*** Implement AI tools for real-time tracking of your marketing efforts, allowing for quick adjustments based on what's working best.

AI Tools for Social Media and Online Marketing

Leveraging AI for Social Media Engagement: Tools like Buffer and Hootsuite use AI to optimize posting times, analyze engagement data, and suggest content improvements to increase follower interaction on platforms like Twitter, Facebook, and Instagram.

AI in Email Marketing: Services such as Mailchimp employ AI to segment email lists, personalize messages, and optimize send times, enhancing the effectiveness of email campaigns aimed at promoting your book.

Online Advertising with AI: Google Ads and Facebook Ads use AI algorithms to target potential readers based on their interests, search behavior, and previous interactions with similar content, ensuring your book ads are seen by those most likely to be interested.

CHAPTER 9: ENGAGING YOUR AUDIENCE WITH AI-CREATED CONTENT

Once your marketing strategy is in place, the focus shifts to creating engaging content that keeps your audience interested and builds anticipation for your book. AI offers tools to generate promotional material and maintain an active online presence.

Generating Promotional Material with AI

Creating Varied Promotional Content: AI can generate a range of promotional materials, from blog posts highlighting the themes of your book to social media snippets that tease plot points or character insights.

Designing Visual Content: Use tools like Runway, Midjourney, Canva or Dall-E to create compelling visuals, including book trailers, promotional graphics, and other visual content that can be shared across social media and your website to capture potential readers' attention.

Customizing Content for Different Platforms: AI can help tailor your promotional content for the nuances of each social media platform, optimizing for the unique format and audience of each.

Using AI to Maintain an Online Presence and Engage with Readers

Automating Social Media Interaction: Tools like Chatfuel or ManyChat can create AI-powered chatbots for your social media pages, answering reader questions, providing book updates, and maintaining engagement automatically.

Content Scheduling and Analytics: AI-driven tools analyze the performance of your content across platforms, suggesting the best times for posting and the types of content that generate the most engagement, helping you to maintain a consistent and effective online presence.

Personalized Reader Experiences: AI can analyze individual reader preferences and interactions to offer personalized recommendations, from suggesting your book based on their reading history to tailoring email marketing messages to their interests.

Let's take a tour of some of the AI driven social-media tools available online:

- *ClickUp:* Best known for project management, ClickUp includes an intuitive AI writing assistant, making it a versatile tool for social media strategy and content creation.

- *SocialBee:* An all-in-one social media management platform that leverages AI for content generation, scheduling, and publishing, supporting a wide range of social media platforms.

- *Canva:* Offers an AI image generator feature, perfect for creating visually appealing social media graphics with ease. Canva supports a wide range of design tasks from social media posts to presentations.

- *Buffer:* Tailors posts to each channel and is known for its effective scheduling and campaign management capabilities, ensuring that your content reaches the right audience at the right time.

- *Flick:* Specializes in turning content ideas into multiple posts, ideal for maximizing your content's reach and engagement across platform
- *Audiense:* Provides intelligent social listening on Twitter, offering in-depth data analysis to better understand and engage with your audience.

- *Hootsuite:* Offers a variety of AI post prompts, assisting in generating diverse and engaging content for social media campaigns.

By harnessing AI in your marketing and promotion efforts, you can create a dynamic strategy that adapts to the market and your audience, ensuring your book reaches its full potential. AI not only streamlines the process but also introduces a level of precision and personalization that traditional methods struggle to match, paving the way for deeper connections with your readers and ultimately, a more successful book launch.

CHAPTER 10: EMERGING TRENDS IN AI AND PUBLISHING

The integration of AI into publishing is not a passing trend —it's an ongoing evolution that promises to reshape the landscape of writing, editing, publishing, and marketing. As we look to the future, understanding the trajectory of AI developments and preparing for what's next is crucial for authors who wish to stay ahead.

Future Developments in AI for Authors

Advancements in Natural Language Processing (NLP): NLP technologies will become more sophisticated, enabling even more nuanced understanding and generation of human-like text. This will enhance AI's role in content creation, making it a more powerful tool for drafting, editing, and even translating books.

AI in Personalized Reading Experiences: Expect AI to play a bigger role in creating personalized reading experiences for audiences. From customizable narratives where readers choose the storyline outcomes to AI-curated reading lists tailored to individual preferences, the reading experience is set to become more interactive and personalized.

Automated Publishing Platforms: The future may see the rise of fully automated publishing platforms, where AI handles everything from manuscript formatting and cover design to distribution and marketing, streamlining the publishing process to an unprecedented degree.

AI-Driven Market Analytics and Prediction Models: Enhanced predictive models will offer authors and publishers deeper insights into market trends, reader preferences, and potential sales volumes, enabling more strategic decision-making from the conceptual phase to post-publication.

Preparing for the Next Wave of AI Innovation

Stay Informed: Keeping abreast of the latest AI developments in publishing is vital. Subscribe to industry newsletters, follow thought leaders on social media, and participate in webinars and conferences focusing on AI.

Experiment and Learn: Don't hesitate to experiment with new AI tools and technologies as they become available. The practical experience will provide insights into how these innovations can be integrated into your work.

Build a Flexible Strategy: As the publishing landscape evolves with AI, so too should your approach. Be prepared to adapt your publishing, marketing, and engagement strategies based on the latest AI capabilities and trends.

Focus on Skill Development: Enhance your skills not just in writing but in areas related to AI, such as data analysis and digital marketing. Understanding the basics of AI and its applications in publishing will allow you to make more informed decisions about incorporating technology into your work.

CHAPTER 11: ETHICAL CONSIDERATIONS AND BEST PRACTICES

As AI becomes more embedded in the publishing process, ethical considerations and best practices must guide its use. Ensuring the responsible use of AI safeguards the integrity of the literary world and maintains trust with readers.

Navigating the Ethical Use of AI in Writing

Transparency: Be transparent about the use of AI in your writing process. If portions of your content were generated or significantly edited by AI, consider disclosing this to your readers.

Copyright and Originality: Respect copyright laws and the originality of content. Use AI as a tool for inspiration and assistance, but ensure that your work remains uniquely yours, avoiding plagiarism and undue reliance on generated content.

Data Privacy: When using AI tools that analyze reader data for insights, ensure compliance with data protection regulations. Maintain the privacy and security of your audience's information at all times.

Ensuring Originality and Authenticity

Human Touch: While AI can enhance your writing process, the core of your work should reflect your unique voice and perspective. Use AI to support and elevate your storytelling, not replace the human element that connects with readers.

Ethical AI Practices: Choose AI tools and services that are committed to ethical practices in AI development and application. This includes transparency in how they operate, respect for privacy, and efforts to mitigate bias.

Creative Integrity: Maintain creative integrity by using AI as a co-creator, not a ghostwriter. Let AI inspire and facilitate your creative process without letting it dictate the direction and essence of your work.

The future of AI in publishing is bright, filled with potential for innovation and growth. By staying informed, prepared, and committed to ethical practices, authors can navigate the evolving landscape with confidence, leveraging AI to not only enhance their work but also deepen their connection with readers in meaningful ways.

CONCLUSION

As we close the pages of "AI Editor: Transforming Words into Wealth," it's clear that the integration of artificial intelligence into the world of publishing is not just a trend but a transformative shift that is reshaping the landscape of writing, editing, publishing, and marketing. This journey through the realms of AI has unveiled its potential to be a powerful ally for authors, offering tools and insights that can elevate the quality of their work, streamline the publishing process, and connect with readers in unprecedented ways.

Summarizing Key Takeaways:

- ***AI as a Creative Partner:*** From generating ideas and drafting content to refining narrative structures and character development, AI can act as a collaborator, enhancing the creative process while allowing authors to maintain their unique voice and vision.

- ***Efficiency in Editing and Formatting:*** AI-powered tools offer significant advantages in editing for grammar, style, and coherence, as well as in formatting manuscripts for publication, saving authors time and ensuring a professional finish.
- ***Strategic Marketing and Promotion:*** The application of AI in marketing strategies and audience engagement has the potential to revolutionize how authors connect with readers, making promotional efforts more targeted, effective, and engaging.

- ***Navigating the Future with AI:*** Staying informed about emerging AI trends and preparing for the next wave of innovation is crucial for authors who wish to remain competitive and relevant in a rapidly evolving publishing environment.

- ***Ethical Considerations:*** Embracing AI requires mindfulness about ethical considerations, ensuring that the use of technology respects copyright, originality, and the authentic relationship between authors and readers.

As you embark or continue on your publishing journey, I encourage you to view AI not as a replacement for human creativity but as a tool that amplifies it. The potential of AI in publishing is vast, but its true value lies in how you choose to integrate it into your work. Embrace AI with curiosity, openness to learning, and a commitment to ethical practices. Experiment with different tools, learn from the insights they provide, and let them inspire you to explore new creative horizons.

Remember, the essence of a great book lies in its ability to connect with readers, evoke emotions, and inspire thoughts. AI can help you achieve these goals in ways that were once unimaginable, but the heart of your story remains uniquely human. Let AI be the wind beneath your wings, propelling your stories to new heights and into the hearts of readers around the world.

The future of publishing with AI is not just about adapting to change; it's about seizing opportunities to create, innovate, and tell stories that resonate across the digital and physical realms. As you move forward, take the lessons and insights from this book with you, and let them guide you in transforming your words into wealth, one AI-enhanced step at a time.

APPENDICES AND RESOURCES

Glossary of AI and Publishing Terms

Algorithm: Set of rules or instructions given to an AI or computer program to perform tasks or solve problems.

Algorithmic Editing: Using algorithms to automate the editing process for text.

Artificial Intelligence (AI): Simulation of human intelligence processes by machines, especially computer systems.

Big Data: Extremely large data sets analyzed computationally to reveal trends, especially regarding human behavior.

Blockchain: System for recording information in a way that makes it difficult to change, cheat, or hack.

Book Formatting Software: Tools that assist in formatting the interior layout of books for print and digital formats.

Book Marketing Tools: Software or platforms designed to help authors promote their books.

Chatbot: AI program simulating interactive human conversation using predetermined responses or text generated by AI.

Content Management System (CMS): Software to manage digital content without needing technical knowledge.

Cover Design Software: Applications designed to help authors or designers create book covers.

Data Analytics: Process of analyzing raw data to find trends and answer questions.

Deep Learning: Machine learning technique that teaches computers to do what comes naturally to humans: learn by example.

Direct Publishing Platforms: Websites or services that allow authors to publish their works directly to consumers.

E-book: Electronic version of a printed book that can be read on digital devices.

E-book Distribution Services: Companies that distribute digital books to various retailers and libraries.

Generative AI: AI capable of generating content like text, images, and music from data it has been trained on.

ISBN (International Standard Book Number): A unique identifier for books, intended to be used commercially.

Machine Learning (ML): Subset of AI enabling software to become more accurate in predicting outcomes without being explicitly programmed.

Metadata: Data that provides information about other data, crucial for organizing and discovering books.

Natural Language Processing (NLP): AI's understanding, interpretation, and generation of human language.

Predictive Analytics: Use of historical data, statistical algorithms, and ML to predict future outcomes, useful in market analysis.

Print on Demand (POD): A printing technology and business process where books are not printed until an order has been received.

Reader Analytics: Data analysis tools that provide insights into reader preferences and behaviors.

Reinforcement Learning: ML where an algorithm learns to make decisions through actions and outcomes.

Royalty Management: The process of tracking and managing payments made to authors based on sales of their books.

SEO (Search Engine Optimization): Practice of increasing the quality and quantity of website traffic through organic search engine results.

Sentiment Analysis: NLP technique to determine sentiment behind words, for assessing opinions.

Self-Publishing Consultants: Professionals who offer advice and services to help authors navigate the self-publishing process.

Supervised Learning: ML approach where models are trained on a labeled dataset.

Unsupervised Learning: Training models on data without labeled responses, allowing the model to identify patterns.

FAQs

- ***Can AI write a book for me?***
AI assists in content generation and idea brainstorming but requires human oversight for originality and coherence.

- ***Is using AI in publishing ethical?***
Yes, when used responsiblyand transparently, especially regarding content generation and data analysis.

- ***How does AI help in marketing my book?***
AI analyzes data to optimize marketing strategies, target audiences, and generate promotional content.

- ***Will AI replace human authors?***
No, AI serves as a tool to support and enhance the creativity and efficiency of human authors.

- ***What are the benefits of using AI in editing?***
AI can speed up the editing process, improve grammar and style, and ensure consistency across the manuscript.

- ***How can I use AI for cover design?***
Tools like Dall-E can generate unique cover images based on textual descriptions, enhancing the book's visual appeal.

- ***Can AI predict the success of my book?***
AI can analyze market trends and reader preferences to give insights, but predicting success involves many variables.

- ***How can AI assist in audience engagement?***
AI can personalize marketing messages, manage social media interactions, and help create content that resonates with the target audience.

● ***What ethical considerations should I keep in mind?***
Ensure the originality of AI-generated content, respect copyright laws, and be transparent about AI's role in your work.

List of AI Tools and Resources

Content Creation and Idea Generation

- *ChatGPT (OpenAI):* Excelling in generating text based on prompts, ChatGPT is invaluable for brainstorming, drafting, and overcoming creative blocks.

- *ShortlyAI:* Offers a focused environment for writing, with AI-driven suggestions to help flesh out stories or articles, making it ideal for writers seeking minimal distractions.

- *Jasper:* Known for its versatility in content generation, Jasper can assist in writing blog posts, social media content, and even book chapters with a user-friendly interface.

- *Sudowrite:* Sudowrite acts as a writing partner that offers suggestions, helps overcome writer's block, and refines prose. It's particularly useful for fiction and creative writing, providing synonyms, rewriting paragraphs, and suggesting plot developments.

- *Grammarly:* Grammarly is a widely-used tool for grammar checking, style improvement, and plagiarism detection. It uses NLP to understand the context of sentences, making it invaluable for editing and refining manuscripts.

- *INK:* INK is tailored for SEO content creation but is also useful for authors looking to optimize their online presence. It uses NLP and ML to suggest improvements that can increase a piece's visibility on search engines.

- *Quillbot:* Quillbot is a paraphrasing tool that helps rewrite sentences or paragraphs to enhance clarity or alter tone. It's beneficial for editing and refining content, ensuring readability and engagement.

- *Writesonic:* Writesonic specializes in marketing content creation, including landing pages, ad copy, and product descriptions. It can also assist authors in generating promotional materials and summaries for their books.

- *Writer:* Utilizes the Palmyra LLM, focusing on transparency and security. It's designed for legal compliance, style guide adherence, and offers a fact-checking feature to ensure content accuracy. This tool is particularly beneficial for companies looking to maintain a specific brand voice across all written content.

- *Rytr:* Known for its solid free plan and affordable high-volume options, Rytr includes basic AI art generation in every plan, making it a cost-effective choice for individuals and small businesses looking to explore AI-generated content and images.

- *Longshot AI:* Stands out for its fact-checking system, aiming to solve the issue of AI-generated content's accuracy. It's a complex software offering document editing, topic research, and quality of life tools to enhance content creation and ensure factual correctness.

- *Nyle AI:* Tailored for eCommerce businesses, Nyle AI uses GPT-3 to generate content focused on short-form copywriting. It includes over 15 short-form templates and features like an image enhancer and influencer research, providing a comprehensive toolkit for online store owners

Image Generation and Design

- *Dall-E:* Creates unique images from textual descriptions, useful for book covers and promotional materials.

- *Visme:* Known for its text-to-image generation tool, Visme offers a broad spectrum of output styles, including photos, paintings, pencil drawings, and more, making it a versatile choice for creators looking to merge AI graphics with content types like infographics and social media posts

- *Midjourney:* Distinguished by its ability to generate digital artwork that resembles hand-drawn illustrations rather than photorealistic images, Midjourney is perfect for creating 'pretty' images like gothic architecture and fantasy landscapes

- *Canva's Magic Write & Design with Text to Image:* Integrates AI-driven design and content creation, allowing for easy generation of marketing materials, social media graphics, and book covers with text-to-image features.

- *NightCafe AI:* Tailored for digital art creation, NightCafe AI offers detailed customization for AI-generated art, making it suitable for both beginners and experienced artists looking to explore digital creativity.

- *DeepArt:* Specializes in transforming photos into artworks based on various artistic styles, ideal for authors seeking distinctive visuals for their projects.

Editing and Proofreading

- *Grammarly:* Offers comprehensive feedback on writing

errors, style, and tone improvements, suitable for a broad range of writing tasks.

- *Hemingway Editor:* Focuses on enhancing clarity and readability by identifying complex sentences and suggesting simplifications.

- *ProWritingAid:* Provides detailed writing reports, highlighting areas like repetitiveness, vague wording, sentence length variation, and more, making it a robust tool for in-depth editing.

- *Antidote:* Offers both online and local proofreading capabilities, supporting English and French. It's praised for its extensive reports and is a great choice for those concerned about privacy and data security.

- *Quillbot:* While primarily a paraphrasing tool, Quillbot also features a grammar checker and citation generator, making it useful for academic works and essays. It's celebrated for its ease of use and the range of tools beyond proofreading.

- *Ginger Software:* Provides a cost-effective option for proofreading, supporting 60 languages. It's beneficial for those needing a basic grammar and spell check across various devices.

- *WhiteSmoke:* Known for its affordability and support for 55 languages, WhiteSmoke offers a comprehensive solution that includes grammar and spelling checks. It works with most browsers and operating systems.

SEO and Content Optimization

- *MarketMuse:* Uses AI to analyze content and offer

recommendations on how to improve for better search engine rankings and reader engagement.

- *SurferSEO:* Focuses on optimizing online content with real-time SEO guidelines, helping writers create more searchable and visible web content.

- *Clearscope:* Offers easy-to-use content optimization based on current SEO best practices, making it suitable for bloggers and content marketers.

- *Alli:* AI focuses on automating SEO tasks like meta tags optimization, link descriptions, and image alts, making it easier for SEO teams to manage campaigns without needing developers or coding knowledge. It integrates with popular content management systems, offering custom automation for on-page optimizations.

- *RankIQ:* suggests titles and content for posts, offering a list of high-traffic, low-competition keywords. It helps create blog post outlines quickly, aiming to rank your content on the first page of Google.

- *Frase:* simplifies SEO content research and optimization, helping users create thorough content briefs and compare their content to competitors'. It aims to make publishing Google-friendly content easier by providing an easy-to-use text editor and competitor analysis.

- *Diib:* offers growth plans and alerts for SEO, social, mobile, and visitor experience optimization. It provides competitor monitoring, keyword tracking, and new content ideas to enhance your SEO strategy.

- *Outranking:* Outranking automates content creation targeting organic traffic through SERP analysis. It provides tools for creating SEO-focused content, such as outlines, briefs, titles, and optimizing existing articles for better search engine performance

Marketing and Promotion

- *CopyAI:* An AI-powered tool designed to generate marketing copy and content ideas quickly, from email marketing to ad copy and product descriptions.

- *Writesonic:* Specializes in creating marketing content, including landing pages, ads, and emails, with specific templates for various marketing needs.

- *Lumen5:* A video creation platform that uses AI to transform text content into engaging video content, perfect for promotional efforts on social media.

- *Hootsuite's free AI tools*: offer a suite of content creation aids, including caption and bio writers, username idea generators, and AI hashtag generators, optimized for social media across multiple languages, making it ideal for content creators and small businesses starting their social media journey.

- *Persado Motivation AI*: An enterprise-level Generative AI platform, perfect for generating high-converting digital marketing messages. It personalizes messages to drive engagement, using a comprehensive knowledge base of consumer motivations and an experimentation engine for language and creative permutations.

- *Personalize:* Personalize leverages AI to track customer preferences, helping businesses promote the right products at the right time. Its real-time insights and personalized campaign capabilities can significantly boost email open rates and click rates.

Self-Publishing Platforms

- *Apple Books for Authors:* Apple's self-publishing platform enables authors to publish e-books directly to the Apple Books Store, providing access to readers who use Apple devices.

- *Barnes & Noble Press:* This platform allows authors to publish both e-books and print-on-demand books, with distribution on Barnes & Noble's online store, giving authors access to millions of readers.

- *BookBaby:* A comprehensive service that provides e-book distribution, print-on-demand, and custom book printing, along with additional marketing and promotional services.

- *Draft2Digital:* Known for its user-friendly interface, Draft2Digital offers e-book and print book distribution to a network of online retailers and library services.

- *IngramSpark:* A favorite for authors looking to reach a wide audience, IngramSpark provides access to Ingram's extensive distribution network, which includes independent bookstores and libraries.

- *Kobo Writing Life:* Kobo offers an easy way for authors to publish e-books and reach readers in over 190 countries through the Kobo Books platform.

- *Lulu:* Offers various self-publishing services, including e-book and print-on-demand options, with the ability to reach audiences across multiple retailers.

- *Amazon Kindle Direct Publishing (KDP):* The largest and most popular platform for self-publishing e-books and paperbacks, offering worldwide distribution and the option for authors to earn up to 70% royalties on sales.

- *Reedsy:* An online platform that connects authors with professional editors, designers, and marketers to help prepare their book for self-publishing on various platforms.

- *Smashwords:* A veteran in the self-publishing domain, Smashwords offers distribution to major e-book retailers and provides authors with various tools for marketing and sales tracking.

Social Media and Content Management

- *ClickUp:* Best known for project management, ClickUp includes an intuitive AI writing assistant, making it a versatile tool for social media strategy and content creation.

- *SocialBee:* An all-in-one social media management platform that leverages AI for content generation, scheduling, and publishing, supporting a wide range of social media platforms.

- *Canva:* Offers an AI image generator feature, perfect for creating visually appealing social media graphics with ease. Canva supports a wide range of design tasks from social media posts to presentations.

- *Buffer:* Tailors posts to each channel and is known for its effective scheduling and campaign management capabilities, ensuring that your content reaches the right audience at the right time.

- *Flick:* Specializes in turning content ideas into multiple posts, ideal for maximizing your content's reach and engagement across platform

- *Audiense:* Provides intelligent social listening on Twitter, offering in-depth data analysis to better understand and engage with your audience.

- *Hootsuite:* Offers a variety of AI post prompts, assisting in generating diverse and engaging content for social media campaigns.

Recommended Reading and Tutorials

AI in Education and Ethics

Horner, E.M. (n.d.). How to Use Artificial Intelligence to Bolster Students' Creativity. Education Week.

Rafner, J., Beaty, R.E., Kaufman, J.C., et al. (2023). Creativity in the age of generative AI. Nature Human Behaviour, 7, 1836–1838.

Sherson, J., et al. (2023). Anthropomorphism of AI in Learning Environments: Risks of Humanizing the Machine.

Thomsen, B.S., et al. (n.d.). The Danger of Equating AI With Humans. EdSurge News.

Self-Publishing Resources

Draft2Digital. (n.d.). Simplify your self-publishing process with Draft2Digital.

Kobo Writing Life. (n.d.). Explore international ebook market with Kobo Writing Life.

PublishDrive. (n.d.). Reach over 400 stores and 240,000 libraries with PublishDrive.

StreetLib. (n.d.). Go global with your self-publishing efforts using StreetLib.

XinXii. (n.d.). Distribute your work in German-speaking countries and beyond with XinXii.

Writing and Creativity Platforms

Birss, D. (n.d.). Learn AI Prompt Engineering - Experiments in Creativity with Dave Birss.

Verb. (n.d.). Verb.ai: A minimalist AI writing tool for discovery writers.

Writing Communities and Forums

Catapult: Don't Write Alone. (n.d.). Grow your writing skills with Catapult's dedicated blog.

The Write Practice. (n.d.). Practice your writing skills with every post on The Write Practice.

The Writing Cooperative. (n.d.). Join a community dedicated to improving writing skills at The Writing Cooperative. writingcooperative.com

Writer Unboxed. (n.d.). Dive into the craft and business of fiction writing with Writer Unboxed.

Writer's Digest. (n.d.). Access a century's worth of writing resources at Writer's Digest.

Writers Write. (n.d.). Enhance your writing practice with resources from Writers Write.

Writing.com. (n.d.). An all-inclusive community for writers of all levels at Writing.com.

Educational Platforms and Communities

Coursera and Udemy. Courses on AI and Machine Learning: Platforms offering tailored courses for learning about AI applications in writing and creativity.

Reddit Communities like r/MachineLearning, r/Artificial, and r/writing. For discussions on AI and writing advice.